NEW YORK
GIANTS

BY TONY HUNTER

SportsZone

An Imprint of Abdo Publishing
abdobooks.com

abdobooks.com

Published by Abdo Publishing, a division of ABDO, PO Box 398166, Minneapolis, Minnesota 55439. Copyright © 2020 by Abdo Consulting Group, Inc. International copyrights reserved in all countries. No part of this book may be reproduced in any form without written permission from the publisher. SportsZone™ is a trademark and logo of Abdo Publishing.

Printed in the United States of America, North Mankato, Minnesota
042019
092019

Cover Photo: Brad Penner/Panini/AP Images
Interior Photos: G. Newman Lowrance/AP Images, 4; Scott Boehm/AP Images, 6, 43; David Stluka/AP Images, 9; AP Images, 11, 15, 17, 21; Pro Football Hall of Fame/AP Images, 13; John Rooney/AP Images, 18; Focus on Sport/Getty Images, 23; NFL Photos/AP Images, 24; Focus on Sport/Getty Images Sport Classic/Getty Images, 26; Al Messerschmidt/ AP Images, 29, 31; Ed Reinke/AP Images, 33; Allen Kee/AP Images, 35; David Duprey/AP Images, 37; Bill Kostroun/AP Images, 38; Damian Strohmeyer/AP Images, 41

Editor: Patrick Donnelly
Series Designer: Craig Hinton

Library of Congress Control Number: 2018965645

Library of Congress Cataloging-in-Publication Data

Names: Hunter, Tony, author.
Title: New York Giants / by Tony Hunter
Description: Minneapolis, Minnesota: Abdo Publishing, 2020 | Series: Inside the NFL | Includes online resources and index.
Identifiers: ISBN 9781532118593 (lib. bdg.) | ISBN 9781532172779 (ebook) | ISBN 9781644941133 (pbk.)
Subjects: LCSH: New York Giants (Football team)--Juvenile literature. | National Football League--Juvenile literature. | Football teams--Juvenile literature. | American football-- Juvenile literature.
Classification: DDC 796.33264--dc23

TABLE OF
CONTENTS

CHAPTER 1

GIANT
KILLERS

The New York Giants had already shocked the world once when they defeated the previously unbeaten New England Patriots in the Super Bowl after the 2007 season. When the teams met in the Super Bowl again four years later, a similar feeling was in the air.

New York finished the regular season at 9–7, a record worse than that of every previous Super Bowl champion. But the Giants got hot at the right time. They won three straight playoff games, including road wins over the Green Bay Packers and the San Francisco 49ers. They now had their toughest test in the Patriots.

New England had a 13–3 regular-season record and was one of the best teams in the National Football League (NFL).

Eli Manning led the Giants to two road playoff victories after the 2011 season.

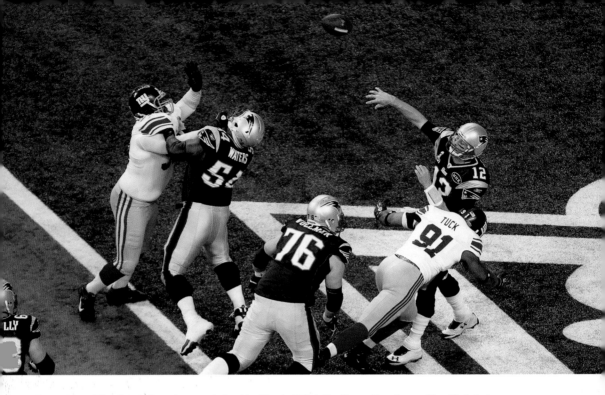

✗ Giants defensive end Justin Tuck (91) hits Tom Brady as the Patriots quarterback throws the ball away, resulting in a safety.

The Patriots had held that status for the previous decade, dating back to when Tom Brady took over as the team's starting quarterback. A Patriots victory would be their fourth Super Bowl title in 11 years.

New York had made it to the Super Bowl thanks to a strong defense. The Giants' success began on the line with defensive end Jason Pierre-Paul. He was an All-Pro player during the 2011 regular season with 16.5 sacks in 16 games played.

The defense came out strong against New England. On the Patriots' first play from scrimmage, Brady struggled to find an open receiver. He threw the ball away to avoid a sack, but he was called for intentional grounding. The penalty took place in the end zone, giving the Giants a safety and a 2–0 lead.

On the next drive, the New York offense had its chance to show off. The Giants went right down the field, and quarterback Eli Manning capped the drive with a 2-yard touchdown pass to wide receiver Victor Cruz. The Patriots offense had been on the field for just one play and the underdog Giants led 9–0.

That lead wouldn't last long. Brady and the Patriots quickly showed why they were one of the NFL's best teams that season. After kicking a field goal to make it 9–3, New England finished the first half strong. The Patriots scored a touchdown with 15 seconds to go in the first half to take a 10–9 lead.

New England struck again on the first drive of the second half, with Brady throwing his second touchdown pass of the game to increase the Patriots' lead to 17–9. The Giants needed their offense to pick up the pace. And slowly but surely, it did. Their next two drives ended in Lawrence Tynes field goals, and New York trailed 17–15 as the fourth quarter began.

The Giants stopped Brady and the high-powered Patriots offense twice. New York's offense had one final chance, taking over at its own 12-yard line with 3:46 remaining.

On the first play of the drive, Manning threw up a deep pass down the left sideline. Wide receiver Mario Manningham was there. He caught the ball and then snuck two feet in bounds before being knocked down by a defender. The 38-yard completion gave New York the ball at midfield.

With a reliable kicker who had already made two field-goal attempts, the Giants only needed about 15 more yards to get into Tynes's range. But they didn't settle for a field goal. Manningham caught two more passes for 18 total yards. Manning also hit wide receiver Hakeem Nicks twice for another 18 yards. Bulldozer running back Ahmad Bradshaw blasted

✖ Ahmad Bradshaw scores the Super Bowl–winning touchdown.

up the middle for 7 yards, then took it to the end zone from
6 yards out. With just under a minute left, the Giants led
21–17. They just needed to stop Brady and New England one
more time.

The Patriots reached midfield and ended up with time for
one Hail Mary pass to the end zone. But Brady's long pass fell
incomplete. It was over. Once again, New York had pulled off
an upset against New England. It was the Giants' fourth Super
Bowl victory. Though there had been some tough times over
the years, New York fans had plenty of reasons to celebrate.

CHAPTER 2

EARLY NFL
POWERHOUSE

New York businessman Tim Mara purchased the Giants for $500 in 1925. Could he have possibly imagined that the value of the franchise would be placed at $3.3 billion nearly a century later? It's unlikely, particularly since the Giants were threatened with extinction before their first season was over.

Mara had lost an estimated $40,000 and needed a big crowd for the last home game of the season to save the team. Fortunately for Mara, star running back Red Grange was in town with his Chicago Bears. More than 70,000 people paid their way into the Polo Grounds, the Giants' home stadium, to watch Grange, one of the NFL's first stars. The huge crowd gave Mara money and hope that New York could indeed support an NFL team.

Giants center Mel Hein receives a watch from NFL President Joseph Carr for being named the 1938 NFL MVP.

LEGEND'S SHORT STAY

One of the greatest athletes in history played for the Giants. Born on an American Indian reservation in Oklahoma, Jim Thorpe blossomed into an Olympic track-and-field champion. He also became a professional baseball and football player. He joined the Giants for three games at the end of his career in 1925.

Mara went on to build one of the best teams in the young NFL. The Giants gained a reputation for a strong defense from the start. In 1927 they had 10 shutouts in 13 games to lead the team to an 11–1–1 record and its first championship. Winning soon became a habit. The Giants suffered just three losing seasons through 1944. They played in eight title games in the process.

Perhaps the most noteworthy season was in 1934. The Giants finished 8–5 and scored more than 17 points in only one game. They were considered an unworthy title game opponent for the defending champion Bears, who had won 18 straight games.

The gloom and doom predicted for the Giants appeared justified when they fell behind the Bears 13–3. A freezing rain had turned the Giants' home field, the Polo Grounds, into a slippery mess. Equipment manager Abe Cohen found basketball sneakers for his players at halftime. The improved traction allowed the Giants to score 27 straight points in the

✖ The Giants used a secret weapon—basketball shoes—to defeat the Bears in the 1934 NFL Championship Game.

fourth quarter. They emerged with a 30–13 win that is now known as "the Sneakers Game."

"They were slipping and sliding," said Giants quarterback Harry Newman, describing the Bears' failed attempts to tackle his sneaker-wearing teammates in the fourth quarter. "They couldn't touch anybody."

Another gratifying year was 1938. The Giants surrendered 41 points in losing two of their first three games. After that they allowed just 38 points total and went unbeaten the rest

STANDOUT PLAYER, COACH

Steve Owen did not leave the Giants after spending six years with them as one of the NFL's best defensive tackles. He began coaching the team full time in 1931 and ended up in the Pro Football Hall of Fame.

Owen captained the 1927 title team. But when he took over as coach, his legend grew. He stayed on the job for 23 years. The Giants enjoyed their greatest run of success during Owen's time as coach. He guided them to eight division crowns and two NFL championships while posting a record of 151–100–17.

Owen also proved to be an innovator on the sidelines. Back in those days, players usually competed on both offense and defense. But Owen created a two-platoon system of specialization in which his players remained fresher by playing only half the game.

of the regular season. They gave up only 10 points in their last five games to set up a clash for the title with Green Bay.

The Packers were ahead 17–16 when Giants running back Hank Soar led his team down the field. He carried the ball five times and added a reception to move the Giants into position to score. Then he leaped to grab a pass from quarterback Ed Danowski and dragged a tackler into the end zone for the winning touchdown. The Giants became the first team to win two NFL Championship Games.

New York quarterback Frank Filchock and coach Steve Owen look on during the Giants' 24–14 loss to the Bears in the 1946 NFL Championship Game.

New York experienced its share of frustration, however. The Giants lost showdowns for the league crown in 1933, 1935, 1939, 1941, 1944, and 1946. The team remained strong into the 1950s. But it did not win another title until 1956. That year, the Giants earned one of the most dominant championship-game victories in the history of the NFL.

CHAPTER 3

WIN SOME, LOSE SOME

The Giants of the early 1950s experienced more frustration than the team did in previous decades. They would play well, but not well enough to reach the playoffs. Or they would reach the doorstep of an NFL title, only to have the door once again be slammed in their faces.

The team had lost its last four championship games heading into the new decade. The trend continued in 1950. The Giants reached the playoffs with a 10–2 record. But they fell to the Cleveland Browns in a one-game playoff to decide which team would advance to the NFL Championship Game. And few were shocked when they recorded winning marks in four of the next five years without qualifying

Coach Jim Lee Howell and running back Frank Gifford celebrate the Giants' victory in the 1956 NFL title game.

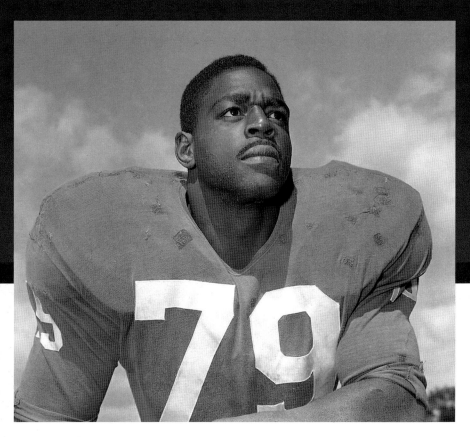

Hall of Fame offensive tackle Roosevelt Brown played for the Giants from 1953 to 1965.

for the postseason. The Giants, however, were compiling a star-studded roster.

The offense featured tackle Roosevelt Brown. He came aboard in 1953 and was named to the All-NFL team eight straight seasons. Halfback Frank Gifford, who also played as a receiver and a defensive back, was chosen for eight Pro Bowls. He racked up 9,862 total yards in his career. Charlie Conerly also emerged as one of the most reliable

RENAISSANCE MAN

Hank Soar played running back and defensive back for the Giants from 1937 to 1944 and then again in 1946. He caught the winning touchdown pass for New York in its 23–17 victory over the Green Bay Packers in the 1938 NFL Championship Game.

But Soar wasn't just a football player, and he did more than dabble in other sports. He participated in professional basketball and baseball after his football career was over—though not as a player.

In the late 1940s, Soar coached the Providence Steamrollers of the Basketball Association of America, which became the National Basketball Association. And from 1950 to the late 1970s, he served as a Major League Baseball umpire, working American League games. He was the first-base umpire in the only perfect game in World Series history, pitched by the New York Yankees' Don Larsen in 1956.

quarterbacks in the league. Meanwhile the defense maintained its strong reputation, led by five-time Pro Bowl defensive end Andy Robustelli.

With several future Pro Football Hall of Famers leading the way, the Giants remained strong. They reached the playoffs in 1956, but they did not perform very well down the stretch in the regular season. The Bears had tormented them in previous title games. Chicago was expected to do the same when the teams clashed for the NFL championship at Yankee Stadium in New York.

Instead, the Giants tormented the Bears. New York's offensive line opened huge holes for the running backs. Conerly threw two touchdown passes. The defense, led by rookie linebacker Sam Huff, held Chicago to 67 rushing yards on 32 carries. The Giants raced to a 34–7 halftime lead and cruised to a 47–7 win for their first title since 1938.

Two years later, the Giants came out on the short end of another NFL title game. However, they did participate in what many consider the most important game in the league's history.

The popularity of the league today is often traced back to the 1958 NFL Championship Game between the Giants and the Baltimore Colts at Yankee Stadium. The star-studded rosters of the two division champions included 17 players who would be inducted into the Pro Football Hall of Fame. A national television audience sat spellbound as the teams played to a 17–17 tie in regulation. For the first time in NFL history, overtime would decide the victor. Hall of Fame quarterback Johnny Unitas engineered the game-winning 80-yard drive. The Colts won it on a 1-yard touchdown run by Alan Ameche.

Baltimore came out on top. But the real winner was the NFL. The league had previously not been as popular as college

✕ Alan Ameche's 1-yard touchdown run gave the Colts a 23–17 overtime win against the Giants in the 1958 NFL title game.

football, but the 1958 NFL Championship Game sparked a surge of popularity that soon led to league expansion, national television contracts, and eventually the creation of the Super Bowl.

Unfortunately for the Giants, the team wasn't in line for the same success—at least in terms of championships. After their 1956 championship season, the Giants compiled a regular-season record of 65–22–3 in the next seven years and qualified for the playoffs five times. But they scored just 50 points in those five championship games and lost them all.

LONG,
HARD ROAD

Perhaps it was the trade of superb linebacker Sam Huff to Washington. Perhaps it was the inability to find a suitable quarterback. Perhaps the Giants had been too good for too long and were simply due for a nosedive. Perhaps it was a combination of many factors. But the bottom line is the Giants began to play bad football in 1964 and continued to play bad football through much of the 1970s.

The team had one last hurrah in 1963 when it nearly won the NFL title. New York had a powerful offense, scoring an NFL-high 448 points (an average of 32 per game), and won the Eastern Conference with an 11–3 record. Quarterback Y. A. Tittle threw for 36 touchdowns, an NFL record at the time, against just 14 interceptions. Pro Bowl selections

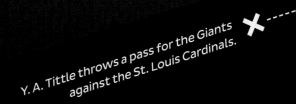

Y. A. Tittle throws a pass for the Giants against the St. Louis Cardinals.

✗ The Giants' Phil King attempts to gain yardage near the goal line in the team's 14–10 loss to the Bears in the 1963 NFL Championship Game.

Del Shofner (64 catches for 1,181 yards) and Frank Gifford (42 catches for 657 yards) were Tittle's favorite targets.

The Giants' defense held up its end of the bargain as well. The unit still had Huff as its leader. Cornerback Dick Lynch also was a key player. He made nine interceptions that season, returning three of them for touchdowns.

On December 29, 1963, the Giants faced a tough, physical Bears team in the NFL Championship Game. The contest was held in frigid, wintry conditions at Wrigley Field in Chicago.

Tittle battled a knee injury throughout the game and had to sit out a few series. Chicago scored two touchdowns on short runs from quarterback Bill Wade. The Bears prevailed 14–10.

In 1964 the Giants fell to 2–10–2, the worst record in the team's history. And in 1966, they sunk even lower with a 1–12–1 mark. The defense that had been a Giants trademark collapsed with the trade of Huff and the retirement of standout defensive end Andy Robustelli. The Giants allowed just 280 points in winning the Eastern Conference in 1963. But they gave up 399 in 1964 and an alarming 501 in 1966. The 1966 season included a 72–41 thrashing by Washington. For one five-week stretch late that season, the Giants surrendered an average of 50 points per game.

Coach Allie Sherman, who had guided the Giants to the playoffs in 1961, 1962, and 1963, survived the bad years.

NO TITLE FOR TITTLE

One of the most successful quarterbacks to wear a Giants uniform owned the unique name of Yelberton Abraham Tittle. It is no wonder he went by "Y. A." The Giants traded for the veteran Tittle in 1961. He led the team to the playoffs in each of the next three years. Tittle's best performance came in 1963, at age 37. He completed 221 passes in 13 games and set a single-season team record—which still stood through 2018—with 36 touchdown passes. Tittle failed to win a championship. But he was inducted into the Pro Football Hall of Fame in 1971.

Fran Tarkenton was a standout quarterback for the Giants from 1967 to 1971.

He managed to raise the team back up to mediocrity. But when the Giants lost their final four games in 1968 and all five preseason games in 1969, he was fired and replaced by Alex Webster.

The new coach didn't do much better. He guided New York to a 9–5 record in 1970. But he recorded two losing seasons in the next three. In 1973, the Giants fell to a disastrous 2–11–1 record and Webster resigned.

The coaching carousel continued to turn. Bill Arnsparger replaced Webster in 1974. John McVay replaced Arnsparger in 1976. Ray Perkins replaced McVay in 1979.

The Giants of the lean years boasted some talented players. They included quarterback Fran Tarkenton, wide receiver Homer Jones, running back Ron Johnson, defensive back Willie Williams, and place kicker Pete Gogolak.

But Tarkenton asked to be traded. He was dealt to the Minnesota Vikings before the 1972 season. The Giants suffered at that important position until Phil Simms arrived eight years later, signaling the start of an era of excellence in New York.

GO, GO, GOGOLAK!

Until the last few decades, most NFL place kickers approached the ball in a forward motion and kicked it with the toe. But by the 1980s, most were "soccer-style" kickers. They moved toward the ball from an angle. The first to use the newer style was Pete Gogolak. He played with the Buffalo Bills of the American Football League (AFL) before being lured away by the Giants in 1966. He was the first player signed by an NFL team after being under contract with an AFL team. It was a move that stepped up the bidding war for players between the two leagues. Gogolak led the Giants in scoring in eight of the nine years he played with them.

CHAPTER 5

SUPER BOWL
SUCCESS

In 1983 longtime owner Wellington Mara grew impatient and promoted untested defensive coordinator Bill Parcells to head coach. The move appeared to backfire right away. A team that had been somewhat successful the previous two seasons went 3–12–1 in Parcells's first season as coach.

But suddenly the Giants blossomed. The team's defense improved rapidly. The offense found a spark in new starting quarterback Phil Simms. The Giants reached the second round of the playoffs in 1984 and 1985. In 1986 they appeared ready for greatness.

Linebackers Lawrence Taylor, Harry Carson, and Carl Banks, nose tackle Jim Burt, and defensive end Leonard Marshall were the standouts on one of the best defenses

Lawrence Taylor (56) was one of the most feared pass rushers of his era.

in the NFL during the 1986 regular season. The Giants gave up the second-fewest points and yards in the league and won their final nine games to finish with a 14–2 record.

The Giants continued to shine in the postseason. They had yet to qualify for the league title game in the Super Bowl era. But they changed that with a 49–3 win over San Francisco and a 17–0 shutout of Washington. The Giants held their two playoff opponents to a combined 374 yards.

All that separated the Giants from an NFL championship were the Denver Broncos. Simms rose to the occasion in Super Bowl XXI on January 25, 1987, in Pasadena, California.

Phil Simms set a Super Bowl record for completion percentage as the Giants beat the Broncos.

He was nearly perfect that day, completing 22 of 25 passes for 268 yards and three touchdowns. Simms was named the game's MVP as the Giants won 39–20. They were Super Bowl champions for the first time.

After stumbling a bit the next two years, the Giants won the NFC East title in 1989. However, they lost to the Los Angeles Rams 19–13 in overtime in their first playoff game. In 1990 the Giants won their first 10 games and allowed just 13.2 points

TERRIFIC TAYLOR

When fans debate the finest linebacker to ever play football, one of the names that gets mentioned is Lawrence Taylor. He recorded more than 10 sacks in seven seasons in a row starting in 1984. He had a league-high 20.5 sacks in the championship year of 1986. His quickness and intensity forced opposing coaches to change their game plans. These attempts to prevent him from dominating their offenses usually did not work. He achieved a rare feat in 1986 when he was selected as the NFL MVP. That award is usually given to quarterbacks and running backs.

"You saw hunger," said San Francisco 49ers Hall of Fame quarterback Joe Montana, who faced Taylor and the Giants in a number of memorable battles throughout the 1980s. "Some guys were great playing their position but didn't have that feeling inside, and that was something [Taylor] had with him every down of every game, and he never lost it."

per game. They defeated Chicago and San Francisco to return to the Super Bowl. The linebacker group, led by Taylor, Banks, and Pepper Johnson, was again the team's strength.

The Giants were forced to play for the NFL championship with backup quarterback Jeff Hostetler. He had replaced the injured Simms in a Week 15 loss to the Buffalo Bills. But Hostetler performed well throughout the playoffs and in the Super Bowl, a rematch with the Bills. The Giants also got 102 rushing yards from running back Ottis Anderson and a strong showing from their defense. However, New York clung

Taylor (56) and Carl Banks (58) carry Bill Parcells off the field after the Giants defeated Buffalo 20–19 in the Super Bowl.

to a 20–19 lead with just four seconds remaining. Buffalo lined up for a potential game-winning field goal. However, Bills kicker Scott Norwood's 47-yard kick sailed wide to the right, and the Giants were again champions.

When he awarded the Super Bowl trophy to his coach, Giants co-owner Tim Mara, a grandson of the original team owner, exclaimed, "Bill Parcells is the best coach the Giants have ever had!"

Parcells retired after that season. The team struggled again until a little-known offensive coordinator named Jim Fassel took over as head coach to right the ship.

CHAPTER 6

BACK ON TOP

The Giants hired Jim Fassel as head coach in 1997. The 48-year-old had been New York's offensive coordinator in 1992 and held the same role in Denver and Arizona over the following years. In his first season with the Giants, the team went 10–5–1 and won the NFC East, but they blew a late lead in the first round of the playoffs and lost to the Minnesota Vikings 23–22.

After two mediocre seasons, Fassel and the 2000 Giants rode a late surge to a long playoff run. Led by defensive end Michael Strahan, running back Tiki Barber, and wide receiver Amani Toomer, the Giants won their final five regular-season games to take the NFC East crown. They routed Minnesota 41–0 in the NFC Championship Game. However, that was the

Tiki Barber played a key role in the Giants' offense during his 10 years in New York.

high point, as they lost 34–7 to the Baltimore Ravens in the Super Bowl.

Fassel got the Giants back to the playoffs once in the next three seasons, but a 4–12 showing in 2003 spelled the end for him in New York. Former Jacksonville Jaguars head coach Tom Coughlin arrived in 2004, as did rookie quarterback Eli Manning. And one year later, the Giants were back in the postseason. Still, critics complained that they were not performing up to their potential.

The 2007 Giants barely reached the playoffs. Many awaited their quick elimination. The Giants responded by upsetting Tampa Bay, Dallas, and Green Bay to again qualify for the Super Bowl.

The Giants displayed a fierce defense in the postseason. Linemen Strahan, Justin Tuck, and Osi Umenyiora had combined for 32 of the team's whopping 53 quarterback sacks in the regular season. Meanwhile, Manning, running back

Michael Strahan celebrates after sacking Tom Brady in the Giants' first Super Bowl win over the Patriots.

Brandon Jacobs, and wide receiver Plaxico Burress led a strong offense. They got hot at the right time. But awaiting them in the Super Bowl were the powerful New England Patriots. The Patriots were attempting to join the 1972 Miami Dolphins as

✗ Odell Beckham Jr. began making acrobatic catches the moment he arrived in New York.

the only teams in NFL history to complete an entire season, including the playoffs, undefeated. Most football fans and media members gave the Giants little chance to win.

The Giants did not care. They held the Patriots to 45 rushing yards and kept star quarterback Tom Brady in check with their furious pass rush. Trailing by four points late in the game,

Manning heaved a long pass that backup wide receiver David Tyree caught, hanging onto the ball by pinning it to his helmet as he was tackled. Four plays later, Burress caught a 13-yard touchdown pass with 35 seconds left to give New York a stunning 17–14 victory.

New York had another strong season in 2008, finishing 12–4 and winning the NFC East. However, the rival Philadelphia Eagles upset host New York 23–11 in the divisional playoffs. The Giants won their first five games in 2009 but slumped to an 8–8 finish and did not make the postseason.

In 2010 New York moved into MetLife Stadium but found itself once again struggling at the end of the regular season. The Giants started 6–2 but finished 10–6 and barely missed the playoffs.

The next season, the Giants went into the postseason with a 9–7

A NEW HOME

MetLife Stadium opened in 2010 as the new home of New York's two NFL franchises, the Giants and the Jets. It was built near Giants Stadium at the Meadowlands in East Rutherford, New Jersey, the Giants' previous home since 1976. Through the 2018 season, the stadium had hosted only one NFL playoff game, a 24–2 Giants victory over the Atlanta Falcons in January 2012. On February 2, 2014, it was the site of the first Super Bowl played outdoors in a cold-weather city. Game time temperatures were near 50 degrees Fahrenheit (10°C) as the Seattle Seahawks throttled the Denver Broncos 43–8.

record and low expectations. However, they finished strong as they once again knocked off the Patriots in the Super Bowl. Manning took home his second Super Bowl MVP trophy after throwing for 296 yards and a touchdown against the NFL's second-worst pass defense.

That proved to be the last hurrah for Coughlin, who couldn't get the Giants back into the postseason the next four years. After the 2015 season, Coughlin resigned, and the Giants promoted offensive coordinator Ben McAdoo to head coach. In his first season, McAdoo led New York back to the playoffs thanks in part to the emergence of Odell Beckham Jr. The young wide receiver had 10 touchdown receptions that year and 1,367 receiving yards. He was selected to that year's Pro Bowl for his strong effort. Unfortunately for New York, that season ended in the wild-card round as the Giants lost to the Green Bay Packers.

McAdoo didn't make it through his second season. The Giants began 2017 with just two wins in their first 12 games and McAdoo was fired. A season-ending injury to Beckham in early October contributed to the team's struggles.

Former Cleveland Browns head coach Pat Shurmur was hired as the Giants' new head coach. With the second pick in

✗ Running back Saquon Barkley had an electrifying rookie season for the Giants in 2018.

the 2018 NFL Draft, New York selected running back Saquon Barkley. He went on to lead the NFL in yards from scrimmage as a rookie and win the league's Offensive Rookie of the Year Award. He rushed for 1,307 yards at an average of 5.0 yards per carry. Barkley also caught 91 passes—an NFL rookie record—for 721 yards, making him only the third rookie to surpass 2,000 yards from scrimmage. With Barkley and Beckham leading the way, the Giants appeared ready to contend for years to come.

TIMELINE

1925
New York businessman Tim Mara purchases an NFL franchise for the city for $500.

1927
The Giants give up just 20 points all season and win their first NFL title with an 11–1–1 record.

1934
The Giants win "the Sneakers Game" 30–13 over the visiting Chicago on December 9 to give New York the NFL championship.

1938
A 23–17 home victory over the Green Bay Packers on December 11 produces another NFL title.

1946
The host Giants lose to the Bears 24–14 in the NFL Championship Game on December 15.

1956
The host Giants clobber the Bears 47–7 on December 30 to win the NFL crown.

1958
New York loses 23–17 in overtime to the visiting Baltimore Colts on December 28 in one of the most storied games in NFL history.

1963
The Giants lose at Chicago 14–10 in the NFL title game on December 29. It is New York's fifth defeat in an NFL Championship Game in six years.

1981
The Giants return to the playoffs for the first time in 18 years and beat the Eagles 27–21 in Philadelphia on December 27.

1983
Bill Parcells is promoted from defensive coordinator to head coach.

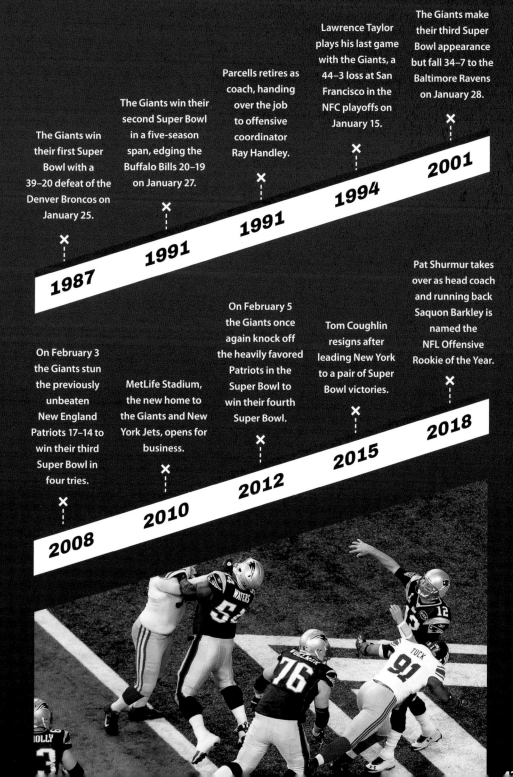

The Giants win their first Super Bowl with a 39–20 defeat of the Denver Broncos on January 25.

The Giants win their second Super Bowl in a five-season span, edging the Buffalo Bills 20–19 on January 27.

Parcells retires as coach, handing over the job to offensive coordinator Ray Handley.

Lawrence Taylor plays his last game with the Giants, a 44–3 loss at San Francisco in the NFC playoffs on January 15.

The Giants make their third Super Bowl appearance but fall 34–7 to the Baltimore Ravens on January 28.

✕
1987

✕
1991

✕
1991

✕
1994

✕
2001

On February 3 the Giants stun the previously unbeaten New England Patriots 17–14 to win their third Super Bowl in four tries.

MetLife Stadium, the new home to the Giants and New York Jets, opens for business.

On February 5 the Giants once again knock off the heavily favored Patriots in the Super Bowl to win their fourth Super Bowl.

Tom Coughlin resigns after leading New York to a pair of Super Bowl victories.

Pat Shurmur takes over as head coach and running back Saquon Barkley is named the NFL Offensive Rookie of the Year.

✕
2008

✕
2010

✕
2012

✕
2015

✕
2018

QUICK STATS

FRANCHISE HISTORY

1925–

SUPER BOWLS
(wins in bold)

1986 (XXI), **1990 (XXV)**, 2000 (XXXV), **2007 (XLII)**, **2011 (XLVI)**

NFL CHAMPIONSHIP GAMES *(1933–69, wins in bold)*

1933, **1934**, 1935, **1938**, 1939, 1941, 1944, 1946, **1956**, 1958, 1959, 1961, 1962, 1963

DIVISION CHAMPIONSHIPS *(since 1970 AFL-NFL merger)*

1986, 1989, 1990, 1997, 2000, 2005, 2008, 2011

KEY COACHES

Tom Coughlin (2004–15):
102–90, 8–3 (playoffs)
Steve Owen (1931–53):
153–100–17, 2–8 (playoffs)
Bill Parcells (1983–90):
77–49–1, 8–3 (playoffs)

KEY PLAYERS *(position, seasons with team)*

Tiki Barber (RB, 1997–2006)
Odell Beckham Jr. (WR, 2014–)
Roosevelt Brown (OT, 1953–65)
Harry Carson (LB, 1976–88)
David Diehl (G/T, 2003–13)
Frank Gifford (RB, 1952–60, 1962–64)
Keith Hamilton (DE/DT, 1992–2003)
Mel Hein (C, 1931–45)
Sam Huff (LB, 1956–63)
Eli Manning (QB, 2004–)
Andy Robustelli (DE, 1956–64)
Phil Simms (QB, 1979–93)
Chris Snee (G, 2004–13)
Michael Strahan (DE, 1993–2007)
Lawrence Taylor (LB, 1981–93)
Amani Toomer (WR, 1996–2008)
Emlen Tunnell (DB, 1948–58)

HOME FIELDS

MetLife Stadium (2010–)
Giants Stadium (1976–2009)
Shea Stadium (1975)
Yale Bowl (1973–74)
Yankee Stadium (1956–73)
Polo Grounds (1925–55)

*All statistics through 2018 season

QUOTES AND
ANECDOTES

Former Giants running back Frank Gifford and quarterback Phil Simms enjoyed highly successful football broadcasting careers after retirement. Gifford was most famous for his role on ABC's *Monday Night Football*, serving as the play-by-play announcer from 1971 to 1985 and as a commentator for another decade. He also covered the Olympics, skiing, and golf for ABC. Simms was the color commentator on the lead NFL broadcast crew for CBS for nearly 20 years. In 2017 he moved from the booth to the studio, where he served as a co-host of the network's *NFL Today* show.

"Winning a championship is bigger than that. It's not a payback or a 'Look at me now' situation. It's a great thing for yourself, but also for your teammates, your ownership, everybody. It's too big of a thing, too important of a thing to give a remark or a comeback."

—Giants quarterback Eli Manning, on answering his critics after leading the team to victory in the Super Bowl in February 2008

To win an NFL MVP Award as an offensive lineman is unheard of in this era of football. But Giants center Mel Hein accomplished the feat in leading the team to a league championship in 1938. Hein set a team record, which has since been matched by quarterback Phil Simms, by playing 15 seasons for the Giants. Hein was an All-NFL selection eight times after the team bid just $150 for his services coming out of college. He never missed a game in high school, college, or professional football. He entered the Pro Football Hall of Fame in 1963.

GLOSSARY

berth
A place in a competition, such as in the NFL playoffs.

contract
An agreement to play for a certain team.

draft
A system that allows teams to acquire new players coming into a league.

franchise
A sports organization, including the top-level team and all minor league affiliates.

Hall of Fame
The highest honor a player or coach can get when his or her career is over.

innovator
One who has new ideas about how something can be done.

line of scrimmage
The place on the field where a play starts.

rookie
A professional athlete in his or her first year of competition.

roster
A list of players that make up a team.

showdown
A long-anticipated battle between two good or great players or teams.

specialization
In football, playing only one position.

MORE INFORMATION

BOOKS

Blumberg, Saulie. *New York Giants*. Minneapolis, MN: Abdo Publishing, 2017.

Bowker, Paul. *Odell Beckham Jr.* Minneapolis, MN: Abdo Publishing, 2018.

Nagelhout, Ryan. *Odell Beckham Jr.: Pro Bowl Wide Receiver*. New York: Britannica Educational Publishing, 2019.

ONLINE RESOURCES

Booklinks
NONFICTION NETWORK
FREE! ONLINE NONFICTION RESOURCES

To learn more about the New York Giants, visit **abdobooklinks.com** or scan this QR code. These links are routinely monitored and updated to provide the most current information available.

PLACE TO VISIT

MetLife Stadium
1 MetLife Stadium Dr.
East Rutherford, NJ 07073
201–559–1515
metlifestadium.com

This 82,500-seat stadium opened in 2010 and houses both the New York Giants and New York Jets. The teams play each other each year during the preseason.

INDEX

ABOUT THE AUTHOR

Tony Hunter is a writer from Castle Rock, Colorado. This is his first children's book series. He lives with his daughter and his trusty Rottweiler, Dan.